Golf Tips

How to Succeed in Golf without really trying

Golf Tips
How to Succeed in Golf
without really trying

Jeff MacNelly
foreword by Dave Barry

TRIUMPH
B O O K S
CHICAGO

Printed in the United States.

This book is available in quantity at special discounts for your group or organization.
For more information, contact:

Triumph Books
601 South LaSalle Street
Chicago, Illinois 60605
(312) 939-3330 Fax (312) 663-3557

Book design and typesetting by Sue Knopf.
Cover design by Salvatore Concialdi.

ISBN 1-57243-327-2

Contents

FOREWORD
by Dave Barry

You've surely noticed that a big golf craze is sweeping the nation, as aging baby boomers discover the benefits of participating in a sport in which the most physically demanding activity is ordering putters by mail.

It has reached the point where, if you don't play golf, your career can suffer. I know mine has. In my newspaper office, the two senior editors—let's call them "Tom Shroder" and "Bill Rose"—regularly go off together during business hours to play golf. I'm sure that while they're out on the "links" whacking their "bogeys," they discuss important business matters and formulate newspaper policies in conversations like this:

TOM: Bill, before I attempt to "shank" this "birdie," I'd like to know your "gut feeling" on the use of quotation marks in the newspaper.

BILL: Tom, I feel they are overused.

TOM: I agree. Let's formulate a policy on that.

BILL: And then let's try on evening gowns.

TOM: Yes! We'll accessorize with brooches!

I'm not saying "Tom" and "Bill" discuss exactly these topics. I'm merely saying that, because I don't play golf, I don't know WHAT they discuss, and so I'm "out of the loop." Perhaps you're "in the same boat." Perhaps you'd like to learn about golf, so that when your colleagues talk about it, you can join in and be "one of the persons." That's why today's topic is Basic Questions About Golf, starting with the question that beginners ask most often:

Q. Has anybody ever used a 9-iron to kill emus?

A. One alert reader sent me a fascinating column written by Ron Henry Strait, outdoor writer for *The San Antonio Express-News;* the column concerns a man named Wes Linthicum, who heads an informal group called the Texas Christian Hunters Association which each year feeds the homeless using donated meat. An area emu farmer offered to give the group a bunch of emus, which are very large, ostrich-like birds. The problem was that the birds were alive, and, as the old folk saying goes, "You can't feed large ostrich-like birds to the homeless if the birds are walking around." The members of the Texas Christian Hunters Association didn't have guns with them, and nobody wanted to strangle the emus manually. According to the column, the problem was solved when:

". . . someone recalled that emus have a tendency to closely examine an object that is dropped on the ground. That's when Linthicum got out his 9-iron . . ."

I called Linthicum, and he told me, after some hemming and hawing, that although the story he'd related to columnist Strait was essentially correct, the golf club part was not one hundred percent accurate in the sense of being true. Linthicum also made these points: (1) If you are ever offered a gift of live emus, you would be wise to turn it down, because "those things have feet like something out of *Jurassic Park*"; (2) If it gets printed in the newspaper that you dispatched emus with a 9-iron, even for a good cause, you're going to hear from some extremely angry animal rights people; and (3) If a person, for whatever reason, did have to dispatch an emu with a golfing implement, it would make more sense to use a wood that an iron.

Speaking of *Jurassic Park,* another question often asked by beginning golfers is:

Q. What happens if a snake eats my balls?

A. Don't worry! The snake will be fine, provided that it gets proper medical care. I base this statement on an article from the July 5, 1996, Harrisburg (Pa.) *Patriot-News,* written by Danielle Hollister, headlined SURGERY GETS SNAKE UP TO PAR. The story states that Sandy and Jeff Paul, who raise chickens, sometimes "put golf balls in their hens' nests to encourage the hens to stay put and lay eggs." One day they noticed a five-foot rat snake near their home with three distinct lumps in its middle, and they realized that the snake had swallowed their golf balls. So they grabbed their 9-iron and . . .

No, seriously, according to the *Patriot-News* article, the Pauls contacted a veterinarian, who successfully removed the golf balls. The snake, which the Pauls named "Spalding," came through the operation OK and has been accepted to law school.

No, I'm kidding about that last part. But I'm not kidding about our final common golf question, which is:

Q. If I do not wish to stand around on a golf course listening to a bunch of business clients drone on about their "mulligans," can I hire somebody to play golf with them for me?

A. Yes! One alert reader sent me a flier for a new Seattle outfit called Golf In Action (We'll Play For You When You Can't). The idea is, you pay a golfer to take your clients out and play with them, thereby (to quote the flier) "giving you the freedom to continue your important daily business needs." I called Golf In Action and spoke with the founder, who told me that her idea has gotten a good public response, although a lot of the calls are from people who want to join her staff and get paid to play golf.

Me, I love the idea of paying somebody to play golf with your clients, and I'm thinking: Why not take it further? Why not pay somebody to have meetings with your clients, and take your clients to dinner, and smoke cigars and drink brandy with your clients, and then throw up on your clients' shoes because you hate brandy and cigars? This company could be called: Businesspersons In Action.

So those are your golf basics. Good luck out on the "links," and be sure to say "hi" to my editors, "Tom" and "Bill," who will be easy to spot because they get stuck in the sand traps with those high heels.

GOLF-IMPAIRED:
Bent Rules
& Poor Play

Golf tips from the Perfesser:

Proper hand position on golf club...

Proper hand position before drive...

Proper hand position after drive.

SHOE
BY JEFF MACNELLY

Golf tips from the
Ol' Perfesser:

When executing a particularly difficult
bunker shot onto the green....

it's sometimes very helpful to have your caddy or partner hold the flagstick.

This enables you to judge the distance to the hole a little more accurately,...

and it helps you concentrate on this most tricky shot

without the distraction of a spectator looking over your shoulder.

Anyway, what he doesn't know won't hurt him.

GREAT SHOT

MacNELLY

5

IF GOD HAD MEANT ME TO PLAY GOLF...

HE WOULDN'T HAVE INVENTED THE PAR 5.

GOLF KEEPS ME ON AN EVEN KEEL.

ON THE DAYS WHEN EVERYTHING IS GOING MY WAY, AND I FIND MYSELF IN AN UNUSUALLY WONDERFUL MOOD...

I GET MY CLUBS, HEAD OUT HERE TO THE COURSE...

AND EVEN THINGS OUT.

7

WHY DON'T I GO AHEAD AND PUTT... THEN I'LL BE OUTTA YOUR WAY...

FINE.

RIGHT IN THE CUP, LADIES AND GENTLEMEN!!

LUCKY STIFF.

WELL, YOU KNOW WHAT THEY SAY...

GOLF IS A GAME OF INCHES...

..AND FEET.

9

I DON'T KNOW WHY I BOTHER PLAYING THESE WATER HOLES...

IT WOULD BE EASIER ON MY BLOOD PRESSURE AND MY WALLET...

IF I JUST SET FIRE TO A STACK OF FIVE-DOLLAR BILLS.

BLOOP

I FEEL RIDICULOUS... WHAT AM I DOING WRONG?

IT'S A COMMON MISTAKE THAT A WHOLE LOT OF PEOPLE MAKE:

YOU'RE PLAYING GOLF.

THWICK!

YOU'LL NEED THIS FOR YOUR NEXT SHOT.

I THINK IT WENT OVER IN HERE SOMEWHERE...

I'LL NEVER FIND IT IN THIS JUNGLE

13

15

Shoe By Jeff MacNelly

PRO SHOP

1 PAR 4 381 YDS

CLANG!

WANT TO HIT A BUCKET OF BALLS BEFORE WE TEE OFF?

NAH.

PRACTICE Tee

PRO SHOP

17

18

19

OKAY, NOW KEEP THAT LEFT ARM STIFF...AND GET THOSE HANDS HIGH...

MAKE TWO VEES WITH YOUR THUMB AND FOREFINGERS, AND LINE THEM UP SO THEY POINT OVER YOUR LEFT SHOULDER.

OVERLAP THAT PINKY...NOW KEEP THE KNEES BENT SLIGHTLY, WEIGHT ON THE BALLS OF YOUR FEET...

KEEP YOUR HEAD PERFECTLY STILL!... EYE ON THE BALL!

NOW JUST SWING NATURALLY.

MACNELLY

13

21

22

23

24

SHOE, I'M AFRAID I'VE GOT A BAD CASE OF THE YIPS.

I JUST CAN'T PUTT ANYMORE...I'VE LOST THE OL' TOUCH...

IT HAPPENS TO SOME OF THE BEST GOLFERS... EVEN THEY GET THE YIPS.

IT MUST BE MY NERVES, OR MAYBE IT'S OLD AGE.

OR MAYBE IT'S THAT SIX-PACK YOU POLISHED OFF ON THE FRONT NINE.

PARTNERS IN CRIME:
Wise-Guy Caddies & Know-It-All Buddies

YUP, GOLF TEACHES YOU TO THINK AHEAD.

SO YOU CAN ALWAYS BE IN POSITION FOR YOUR NEXT SHOT.

19th Hole BAR

BUMPKINS...THEY SAY THAT GOLF IS A GAME OF INCHES.

THWACK

THEY MEANT TO SAY IT'S A GAME OF HOURS.

Shoe

By Jeff MacNelly

I DIDN'T SEE WHERE IT WENT.

STRAIGHT AHEAD.

HOW DID THAT HAPPEN?

IT'S RIGHT UP ON THE EDGE OF THE GREEN...

How to outdrive your partner in two easy steps:

1. Pick out a new, very high quality golf ball.

2. Now pick out an old, very low quality partner.

41

42

FORGET IT. YOU NEED THE EXERCISE.

AND BESIDES, A CADDY WILL HELP FIND LOST BALLS...

NO SMALL THING IN LIGHT OF YOUR WILD DUCK HOOK.

WELL, A CADDY MIGHT BE ABLE TO FIND THE BALL...

BUT A GOLF CART WILL NEVER LAUGH AT YOU...

MACNELLY.

I TOLD LOON TO GET US A CADDY AND MEET US AT THE NEXT GREEN.

THERE HE IS NOW, BUT I DON'T SEE ANY CADDY...

THAT'S OUR CADDY?!

DON'T GET SO UPTIGHT...

A '58 WAS ALL I COULD FIND ON SUCH SHORT NOTICE.

MACNELLY

47

48

WHIFF

I KNOW IT'S SORTA SILLY...

THWICK

57

58

THE RIGHT STUFF:
Clubs, Clothes & Carts

67

71

75

Shoe®

By Jeff MacNelly

1 PAR 4 381 YDS

THIS HOLE IS A DOGLEG TO THE LEFT.

LUCKILY, SO IS THIS DRIVER.

MOST GOLFERS PLAY THE COURSE RIGHT DOWN THE FAIRWAY...

IN THE ROUGH:
Sand Traps,
Water Hazards, &
Other Joys of the Game

MOST OF THE TIME CLUB SELECTION IS VERY IMPORTANT IN GOLF.

BUT IN SOME CASES IT DOESN'T MAKE ANY DIFFERENCE...

91

AH, GOLF! THERE'S NOTHING QUITE LIKE THE SWEET CRACK! OF BALL MEETING WOOD...

SLICE

CRACK

WHAT ARE YOU DOING OVER THERE?

TEEING OFF.

IN THE ROUGH?

YEAH, THIS WAY MAYBE I CAN HOOK IT ONTO THE FAIRWAY.

WIGGLE THE FANTAIL A TAD...

KEEP IT ALL LOOSE.

NOW BRING THAT CLUB BACK EASY.

SWIVEL THOSE HIPS.

NOW START DOWN ON THE PERFECT GOLF SWING...

REMEMBERING TO STAY LOOSE AND RELAX EVERYTHING.

—EXCEPT THE GRIP.

97

OH NO!!

By Jeff MacNelly

IN THE SAND AGAIN, PAL...

HITTING OUT OF THE SAND...

ONE OF THE TOUGHEST SHOTS IN GOLF.

YOU HAVE TO HIT DOWNWARD, A FEW INCHES BEHIND THE BALL...

THE NEXT HOLE IS A PAR 4...

OR PAR 24, COUNTING THE WATER PART.

NOW WE'RE COMING TO A WATER HOLE, SO DON'T FREAK OUT.

OH NO...

IT'S NOT VERY FAR TO THE OTHER SIDE.

By Jeff MacNelly

THIS IS A DOG LEG TO THE LEFT...

UNFORTUNATELY, YOUR TEE SHOT WAS A DOG LEG TO THE RIGHT.

NOW THIS IS GONNA BE A REAL TRICKY SHOT.

IT CALLS FOR A WHOLE DIFFERENT STANCE.

104

113

TWENTY SHORT YEARS AGO I WAS IN THE ARMY...

CHOPPING MY WAY THROUGH THICK JUNGLE UP NEAR THE CAMBODIAN BORDER.

TIMES SURE HAVE CHANGED.

THWICK

SORT OF.

TWIK